PRACTICAL SPIRITUALITY

15 Practices to Heal, Awaken and Embody Your High-Vibe Self

Rev. Joya Sosnowski, B.msc., MMT

Published by Legacy Press Books, a subsidiary of S & P Productions, Inc.
311 Main Street, Suite D
El Segundo, CA 90245
310-640-8885
www.legacypressbooks.com

Published and printed in the United States of America.

ISBN 978-1-7329566-3-6

Dedication

The word *thanks* isn't adequate to express the gratitude I have for my husband, best friend, and life partner, Chris, who has never wavered in his support of me. You saw the real me the moment we met. I don't know if I would be where I am now without you, and I love sharing this adventure of life with you. And to my amazingly creative, kind, thoughtful, wise souls and talented children, El and Weston, you have been my greatest teachers and I am honored you chose me to be your mom in this lifetime. I love you with all of my being. And of course, my Naphsha, my higher self, eternally connected to Source, who never stopped communicating with me, even when I didn't have the eyes to see or the ears to hear.

Table of Contents

Introduction

Hello dear reader. This is the book I wish I had come across when I began the process of spiritual awakening, which happened quite unexpectedly. I have always been a seeker of deeper meaning and truth in life but came at it from an intellectual point of view. I have been working on my mindset since 1991.

Spiritual awakening is better defined as a process that always continues, not a destination to get to. It's a deeply personal experience, unique to each person. There is an inner truth that lives within each human being, which calls the person forth; an urge that wants you to stretch and grow continually into something more. This energy is the same energy of consciousness and intention that lives within a seed and urges it into the expression of the fullness of its being. You awaken when you discover this truth within you, and just as the mighty redwood continues to grow as long as it's alive, so too do you.

Your life itself is the path you must walk to the awakening of the truth of who you really are. Your experiences are the lessons you learn and grow from. You and you alone are the only person who can do this work for yourself. No one can tell you exactly what's right for you. It's very experiential. As you learn to listen and trust yourself, you find your way. And then it seems so obvious and so clear, you wonder how you didn't see it before. It's literally like a light turns on and everything just appears clearer. This is enlightenment.

The word awakening is an interesting choice for this process. It indicates there is something asleep in the first place, something dormant or hibernating that already exists within, that wakes up. You can't awaken something that doesn't already exist. If someone was asleep, that means they must have fallen asleep in the first place. Enlightenment, as it turns out, isn't something you find, it is pre-wired in your body. Enlightenment is the normal state. You came here this way. Clear seeing, following and trusting the urge to express yourself.

I believe that the human body is a spiritual technology, and you have everything you need within you to tune into a higher vibrational way of being. There are different aspects of consciousness, and you get to choose your own adventure, thanks to the gift of free will. The apple seed can only become an apple tree, but the seed in you can express its creative nature through you in any number of ways. The purpose of being human isn't in the *doing,* it's in the *being* and actions of creating from love itself.

You are energy. You are a vibration. You are not at all solid, and there is no solid self or what you constantly call "I" either. As you raise your vibration to another frequency, you literally start picking up different information from the quantum field, where all information already exists. Your body is basically an antenna that picks up what resonates with you. When you transform your consciousness, you transform who you're being, and thus, what's outside of you reflects these changes.

You have within you a quantum consciousness energy source Yeshua (Jesus) called the Naphsha, pronounced *noff-sha.* The word Naphsha is an Aramaic word and is used over 200 times in the New Testament. It is translated as the word "soul," but it is so much more than that. I like to think it's the quantum self that is connected and lives energetically in the Source field, and is what scientists call our vital life force. It is individuated as the drop of consciousness called "self" that came preprogrammed with talents, gifts, and personality traits to be used in service of the Naphsha to have a human experience for the soul's growth. This is the same intention and consciousness that is in the seed. We don't have a Naphsha, we are a Naphsha. You can learn to listen to its guidance so that you pick up higher vibrational

2

experiences and ideas from the field that only you can express in a particular way.

In this book, I will give you practices to teach you how to attune to the Naphsha's vibration to allow it to inform your life through your heart, and to allow your brain and ego to be in service of this Self. You will discover more inner peace, joy, awe, reverence, and love than you ever thought possible. You will discover that you can create a literal "heaven on earth."

I have written this book of spiritual awakening for seekers who are ready to find and use the keys to the kingdom. They are indeed within you. This book may seem simple, as all great truths are, but I promise you that if you will practice what is written here your entire life will completely transform in a relatively short amount of time.

Humans are meant to grow and transform slowly to the rhythm and pace of nature. Your heartbeat is your own rhythm of transformation. Know that as you practice what is written in this book, you are slowly being recreated—heartbeat by heartbeat, breath by breath, thought by thought, action by action—becoming new, growing into a new way of being as surely as the water and sunlight coax the sprout out of a seed. The very act of practicing *is* the transformation happening! One of my favorite quotes that illustrate this is by C.S. Lewis: "Isn't it funny how day by day nothing changes, but when you look back everything is different?"

All things that transform must go through a dying and rebirthing process, and as divinely graced human beings, we all get to rebirth and recreate ourselves over and over, breath by breath, thought by thought, action by action, day by day. You are a fluid and a living, radiant expression of creative Source itself. You are a very powerful constant cocreator.

Quantum science now knows that the universe is intelligent and conscious. The field is intelligent; the field is Source Creator and you are an extension of that exact same intelligence. An easier way to understand this is to know that the Divine is all of you, but you are not all of the Divine.

Here's to you opening the spiritual eyes of your mind and heart and developing an unblocked flow between the beautiful loving joy of your Naphsha embodying and expressing more and more through your physical body. In this way, we will all bring heaven to Earth.

Chapter 1

Realization & Awakening

"One day, an older wiser fish swam by two younger fish and said, 'How's the water?' The younger fish were confused and replied, 'What's water?'" ~ David Foster Walter

I love this allegory because it perfectly illustrates awakening. You awaken when you realize you are swimming in the sea, and you are a drop of that sea. It's like a light turns on, so you can see all the ways your life doesn't make sense. Or it can feel like a sudden epiphany, an *aha!* moment.

Maybe you come to realize that what you're doing isn't working anymore. Or you realize that you are now causing yourself more pain than pleasure through habitual behaviors and patterns. You feel stuck, or you just aren't satisfied or happy despite all your outer success and accomplishments.

Realization is recognizing and knowing there is something more than anything already "out there." It's the first thing that must happen to create space for the rising awareness in you to become willing to do what it takes to change.

A crisis happens when you live from just the ego. The ego is the self you call "I" that identifies itself with everything outside itself: the name, the job, the labels, the roles, the things, the titles, the status, the education, the position. It doesn't matter how much you have or how great you've become. Without a connection to the transpersonal self, the Naphsha, all of that is meaningless. There is a feeling of never feeling happy or satisfied and it leads to debt, disease, depression, and addiction when you think the solution to all of your unhappiness is somewhere "out there."

Everything you have is a result or effect of a cause through action. You know what your results are by looking at your own life. Are you satisfied? Content? Joyful? In a state of abundance? Are you free? Do you have inner peace? Do you feel you have a purpose? Do you feel your life has meaning? Are your relationships happy? How's your health?

Your Naphsha, or higher self, is using your life and your experiences to get your attention and wake you up. Everything is right here, right now.

What are the areas or situations you would like to be different? If you could wake up tomorrow and have one thing transformed or healed, what do you imagine that one thing would be? How do you think your life would be different than it is today with that change in place? This image and feeling are the new vibration, the next evolution of you, that you are being called to live into.

Taking Responsibility

Great leaders have demonstrated and shown humanity that our inner thoughts and feelings and our outer responses are totally up to us, regardless of what anyone or anything outside us is doing. Realizing that you're the one responsible for your own life is the hardest step to take. Realizing that your life is a mess or that you are in pain isn't pleasant, but it's powerful.

The invitation from Soul is to greet this dawning awareness with a sense of inquiry, curiosity, and compassion, not more self-judgment or condemnation. Give yourself a break. You simply don't know what you don't know. Maya Angelou said, "When you know better, you do better." Know that by having a realization you have activated the spark of transformation.

All transformation begins with the *willingness* to allow transformation to occur. So, this is an opportunity to give yourself some love, gratitude, and self-kindness for the ways you've coped up to this point in time. If everything is a mess, don't stress! You have begun the process by being honest with yourself. This is a tremendous act of courage.

The Secret: There is Nothing to Change

Are you ready for a huge mindset shift? There is nothing that needs to change. There are only things to accept. What's done is done. Honesty is a massively important part of this work, because the ego likes to trick and lie in its dysfunctional ways to protect you. It's impossible to change anything that has already happened. All you can change now is the story you tell yourself about it, and the meaning from what has happened. Doesn't it feel more relaxing inside to say to yourself, "My life is the way it is because of choices I have made. Since I'm not happy with the outcomes, I must have chosen in error. I am free to choose differently."

Begin to notice the voices that speak to you within. Do they say, "I want," or "I need?" Know that they will fight back against your soul's voice. The ego doesn't want to die. But in order to allow the grace of transformation to occur, the ego needs to be put back in its place, in service of the soul's voice, which comes in through the intelligence of the heart.

Just be in notice of it, and if anything arises, breathe into it and accept it as part of your experience. Ask to see the truth of it, and you will quickly discover that the ego is very much like the Wizard of Oz—

it's a tiny little fragment that is not even real, using a megaphone to get your attention.

The Practice—Who Is This?

In your journal, write honestly about the realization you're having about yourself or your life. Be perfectly honest with yourself.

Answer the questions I asked earlier. Do you believe that this can be transformed? Do you have absolute faith and certainty that your realization is an invitation to live a higher vibration of your life?

What if this was all happening for you and not to you? What are the lessons you have learned and are learning? What strengths have been cultivated in you, or do you imagine will cultivate in you when you're on the other side of it? What are the hidden gifts? Perhaps the answer is simply, "I woke up."

When you notice, the inner narrator saying, "I," begin to ask, "Who is this? Who is the I that's speaking? What does it need or want? You can even ask it: who are you?

Accept and give love to everywhere you are and everything you have created, even if it's a mess right now. Whatever the image is you see of yourself in a different scenario, tune into what that feels like, and journal some ways to change your vibration to become that version of you, or just feel into that energy and say thank you, I am ready and willing. All that's required is a mustard seed-sized bit of faith.

Chapter 2

No Regrets, Just Lessons

*"Self-knowledge is not necessarily
good news."
~ Lily Tomlin*

Right after you have the realization that you need to change
something about yourself or your life, you might find yourself
slipping into regret. Regrets bubble up with realization because they
are part of realizing that we could have been doing things differently.
The brain loves to time travel. It likes to look to the past with
judgment and play the shoulda-woulda-coulda game, and it likes to
fantasize or worry about a future that hasn't happened yet. The point
of regret, however, is not to keep us stuck in a shame spiral, but to be
used as fuel in the present moment to do something different. You can
choose to treat yourself like you would a child. You wouldn't harshly
judge your child for making mistakes. You'd lovingly ask, "What did
you learn from this?"

Regret is dwelling on the past, and there is nothing, absolutely
nothing, you can do to change anything that's already been done. The
way the mind thinks about the past is a perfect reason to learn to put
it back where it belongs: in service of the awakened heart.

Scientists now know that our brains have 60,000+ thoughts a day, and
a whopping 90% of those thoughts are repetitive—they're the same
thoughts you thought about yesterday! The brain creates habits. It
seeks shortcuts. That's what it's made for. It's a habit-forming,
pattern-seeking, meaning-making machine. Your brain cells only
have two functions: activating or inhibiting neurons. Since your brain
takes up most of the energy in your body, it loves to be efficient, so

as your eyes are looking out and your ears are listening, the brain is working, asking itself what is relevant to your views. You literally see and bring to conscious thought only what you already agree with, or what you fear. The brain is very powerful and it also seeks to answer the questions you ask it or tell it. Being stuck in the energy of regret only creates MORE things to be in regret about.

That's why you're a powerful being when you learn to stay present and notice what's going on in the brain-processing machine. You can learn to question your own thinking and tell your brain exactly what you want to notice and create.

Looking at your list from chapter one, what are the regrets arising now? Are they about time wasted, doors you think are closed, damages you've done to yourself or to others? Notice the story you're telling yourself about your experience and again ask, "Who is the "I" saying this?"

Part of regret is healing and patching up what you can right now, with what you have right now. Are there people you need to apologize to? That includes yourself. Make a list. It doesn't mean you have to act on it. It's just to bring it into your conscious awareness. Let this feeling of regret energize you to make a small change today. The next chapter covers forgiveness.

If you don't do something to change what you realized and now regret, what will your life be like next year?

One of the greatest gifts (and one of the most painful) is that we humans learn through duality. That means we often have to see for ourselves what it is that we don't want, so we can know what we do want. We often hurt ourselves to discover how to be kind and gentle to ourselves. Regret is a powerful tool for such learning.

There is always a lesson in everything, and your own life has been a perfect path for your own growth. There are breakthroughs that come from the breakdowns and messages in the mess *if* you can be honest with yourself and see the truth. As they say, the truth will set you free, but first, it will piss you off. Let regrets be a teacher and a fuel to begin to do the work <u>today</u>. Also, know that regret isn't even real. It's a perception based on what your mind is now thinking. *"What could have been, should have been, would have been if only I had done ..."* The truth is things are as they are, and that's the way it is. It doesn't mean you're stuck or that things can never change.

It's not fair to judge yourself for your past actions when you didn't know better. You're always doing the best you can at any given time unless you're aware that you're not and you're choosing not to. Everything is a lesson, a learning experience to grow your own wisdom.

Now that you have a list of regrets you're experiencing, what have you learned from them?

Why are you the one who allowed your life to come to this point? What are the choices you made when you didn't know better? Can you see the wisdom you have now from these learned experiences?

Do these prompts with an attitude of kindness and compassion toward yourself. You don't know what you don't know, and you cannot judge the past with your present eyes. If you knew then what you know now, you would have made better choices. Know that we all do the best we can with the tools we have at every moment of our lives.

Practice Mindful Self-Compassion

The entire point of feeling regret or remorse is to learn a lesson from it. If you beat yourself up, you pile pain on top of the pain you're already experiencing. Regret is simply the fruit of what you've created. It's information, nothing more. The following is a powerful practice that I recommend you do many times a day, anytime you catch yourself speaking unkindly or judging yourself.

Place your hand softly on your heart. Take a deep breath and say the following:

"I offer myself self-forgiveness. I forgive myself for judging myself for the mistakes of my past. Mistakes are simply mis-takes, which means I mis-took a situation, and now have the opportunity to begin again, with more wisdom and experience. Now *I know, I have gained knowledge,* and to apply what I know is to be wise. I am so grateful.

May I be free of suffering.
May my heart be full of love.
May my mind be at ease.
May I have the strength to create a life I love and a self I honor."

I did this practice myself in my own healing journey, until one day, after about a year of saying this many times a day, my own mind called me sweetheart in the midst of a stressful moment. I felt so relieved that the mean voice had gone that I stopped my car and cried tears of joy. I want that for you, too.

CHAPTER 3

Forgive & Release

"In reality, letting go is as simple as opening your hand and letting go. Most people though, spend a lifetime creating more things to let go of."
~ Joya, from my own journaling process

Letting go is the powerful gift of forgiveness. Letting go means freedom. In the ancient texts about forgiveness, forgiveness is not something that happens for the people outside of you, but a process that happens within you. Much like gratitude, forgiveness is an attitude.

Forgiveness is about canceling your disappointments and upsets about what has happened; it's taking back your energy wasted in wanting something or someone to be other than what they are or were. To forgive is to let loose of the ties that bind you. By holding on to stories and the ways you have been hurt, you create a block to new possibilities that want to unfold for you. Energetically you can even keep creating the same situations over and over again. We create from who we are – not from what we say we want. Lessons will be repeated until learned.

Forgiveness never means that what happened is not a big deal or is okay. It doesn't let the other person off the hook, and it certainly doesn't mean you allow that person into your life if they're toxic. In fact, the other person doesn't even need to know you're forgiving them unless you want them to know.

You're the only person responsible for your actions and feelings, which means other people are also the ones responsible for their own actions and feelings. True forgiveness means you're relinquishing the burden of someone else's actions so you can free yourself to live your life. You release the other person to the consequences of their actions instead of carrying the burden for them.

Forgiveness and letting go create tremendous space within you to receive what you want to create. It means to be free from the wrongs of others so you can step into the flow of your own life. This is taking your power back.

Forgiving Yourself

Struggling with regret and forgiveness work can sometimes be more difficult if you're the one who has harmed others or yourself. You are not your past behavior. The person you were before you had your realization and began your awakening process is not the same person you are now, today. The human body recreates new cells constantly. You are literally not the same person as you were 10 years ago. The only things telling you that you are that person are the stories you tell yourself about yourself. Remember there is no solid "I" to speak of!

A lack of self-forgiveness leads to a lifetime of self-punishment through not allowing yourself joy, good relationships, or success. It can be self-sabotage, addiction, depression, insecurity, anger, or creating emotional or physical illness.

Know that you, above all else, deserve your own kindness and forgiveness. On the quantum realm, all potentials happen instantly. There is nothing to forgive and hold onto any longer the moment you feel it, forgive it, and choose to release it.

Feel the love of Naphsha within you. Put your hand on your chest. Feel your heart beating and know that the divine perfection lives in you. You are a temple for this divine aspect to live and express through. Forgiveness clears the space so more of it can live through you.

Deeper Forgiveness Practice

This is a branch from a wonderful forgiveness process I came upon a long time ago from the work of Dr. Edith Stauffer. I use it for myself, and I recommend it to my clients who have a lot of trauma work to do.

- Forgiveness is the decision to not punish the self for the hurts and wrongs of others. It's the choice to be free. Who would you be without the story of wrongs you keep within you?
- Say, "I choose to stop punishing myself and feeling bad for what _____ has done/is doing to me."
- If journaling is powerful for you, you can journal it, and if visualization is powerful for you, you can visualize. Bring to mind the person who has hurt you. Imagine they are sitting with you. Say to them, "I would have preferred that you had done/said/been_____."
- "But the fact is, you didn't do that. I will do it to release this pain and this incident back into the nothing from where it came. I choose to let go and be free of it."
- "I now cancel all demands, expectations, and conditions that you do or say to me now or in the past. I release the demand that you be any way other than you actually are. You are the one responsible for your actions and deeds. I release you now to your own karma."
- Know that this person has a soulful self, just as you do. See if you can summon up compassion for this person, because they are disconnected and blind to their Source. If you can and it feels right, say, "I send light and love from my soul to yours. I release you."

You can do this for every hurt you've experienced from someone else. I know in doing this work for myself, I have forgiven and let myself loose from all the chains I allowed others to bind me with. I carried a lot of trauma pain from the abuses I suffered as a child, and this process not only freed me of other people's burdens, I developed compassion for how sick and twisted their minds are, and how closed off they were to Source.

Their pain is their pain to bear. Let others live with their karma. There is a powerful saying that is very true: hurting people hurt people. Trauma not transformed, gets transferred onto others.

I can share an insight I had around trauma. I felt so much anger that one of the people who abused me passed away, and I was angry that I never got to ask him why he did what he did to me. I heard a voice I believe was my Naphsha say within, "WHY doesn't matter. There is no why because it was never about you. You were just there. It wasn't personal." I can't tell you the relief I felt in that realization. I have forgiven him, that's his burden to carry. Not mine.

You deserve this same level of love and forgiveness so you can be reborn into a totally different version of yourself: the version Source created and is continuing to call forth into expression of being.

Chapter 4

Visioning Possibility

"Whatever your mind can conceive and believe, it can achieve."
~ Napoleon Hill

Realization, regret, and forgiveness work to clear the path for you to literally see yourself, your life, and your possibilities with different eyes. It might seem that what you were doing before now makes no sense and you wonder how you ever thought that was all there was. This stage can feel lonely because you might feel different than you've ever felt before. Your relationships might feel strained because you are literally changing your vibration and when that happens your resonance changes, and what resonated with you before doesn't anymore, including relationships.

It can also feel exciting because it feels expansive, and it's really like having a blank canvas on which to paint a whole new scene for yourself. This is where you begin to attune your inner lowercase self (ego) to your higher self (Naphsha) to create a higher vision for yourself.

It can feel fearful, because the next vibration of yourself is trusting that you can step into a different way of being, even when you don't know what that is yet. Everyone says make friends with your FEAR so I created an acronym: Friendly Expansion & Alignment Reminder.

Looking back, now that you know the lessons regret taught you and you see the strengths it's given you, do you have a sense of everything being mysteriously and perfectly woven together to get you to this point? Do you have a sense of an unchanging self that has always been within you? Can you sense a self that is more than your thoughts, feelings, and personality, a constant self? Describe this self's way of being. It's the awareness that has always been there, observing and witnessing your life.

There is a force in the universe as real as gravity, that Yeshua called the rukha d'koodsha. It's the universal cleanup crew—the energy that comes along behind humanity and sweeps up the messes and turns everything to good. Everything does not happen for a reason! This force helps make reason out of everything that happens, and to use everything that happens to create what is good, holy, and beautiful.

So now you get to play. Get out your journal and let your imagination or your creative imaging faculty dare to put you in the grandest, highest expression of your life. Ask for guidance from your higher self to give you a vision of a new way of being. Close your eyes and allow an image-in of who you are in your ultimate way of being. Don't shut anything out. Why not allow yourself to be the hero in your own story?

Write in your journal about what you sense or see is possible for your life, and what you know to be your unchanging self.

Your higher self is called your Naphsha, which is connected to the field, to the quantum, to Divine love, God, whatever it is you call it. Your Naphsha lives through you to the extent you allow it to. Your ego can get in the way. In AA, ego as an acronym stands for "edging God out." Knowing about the Naphsha and understanding the teachings of Yeshua as I do now, it's a perfect acronym. Every human being has free will, and the soulful self will enter and live through you to the extent that you allow it. Or you can let your ego run the show— it's totally up to you. This allowing comes in the form of intuitive guidance.

Six Ways Your Higher Self Communicates With You

I call these the IGS, your inner guidance system.

- **Intuition** - You experience this as a subtle knowing. You can't explain it, you just know things like walking out the door and sensing your intuition tell you to grab some water, so you do, and then someone needs a bottle of water and you just happen to have one.
- **Auditory** - You hear a little voice that speaks to you.
- **Visual** - You see images and pictures play out in your mind's eye.
- **Hunch** - You experience this through your solar plexus as a gut feeling or hunch that feels like a strong yes or a no.
- **Knowing** - Gnosis, a complete knowing that lands all at once. It's almost like you absorbed a complete scene from a movie and you just know.
- **Signs, symbols and synchronicities** - A butterfly shows up every time you think about a deceased relative, or you think about something and a license plate has the answer. When your eyes are open, these things happen all the time.

How do you notice this connection?

1. Can you think of a time you asked for something, and it arrived in a way you didn't expect, but in a way you understood? Write about that experience. For example, I kept saying I needed a new car, I intended to get a new car, and then my car was stolen! I learned to be more specific with my requests and to ask that they be delivered with grace and ease.
2. How do you identify who you are? Do you use labels such as mom, dad, airline pilot, nurse? Do you identify by personality? By nationality, gender, job, or health status? Which self

is the real you? Are you the same self you were last year? Who do you think you are now? The idea is for you to truly see that you're a changing self. You can therefore change into a self that is aligned with your truth: *You are a spiritual being using and having a human experience for the purpose of your soul's growth.*

3. This vision you have of yourself determines who you think you are and how you live your life. Your vision guides your beliefs and perceptions. You really do see what you believe. Dr. Wayne Dyer said, "When you change the way you look at things, the things you look at change." He was entirely correct; the main thing to change is how to see yourself.

Allowing Your Higher Self to Create Your Vision

This exercise will get you in connection with your inner self, which has a direct connection to your higher self.

- Sit in a comfortable position and bring awareness to your body. What feelings do you experience and where do you feel them?
- Next, bring awareness to your thoughts. Notice your thoughts for as long as you can and when you forget to notice, bring your attention back and notice how the mind wanders where it wants to.
- Bring awareness to the desires and wants your ego has for itself. Don't judge them, just notice. You know they're the ego because they want attention or some other way to feel special or important.
- Now bring your awareness to your physical body. Notice the five senses and what you feel physically. What do you smell or taste? Notice the constantly changing states of the body
- and your own physical changes as you've gone through life.

- And now ask which part of you is the observer of these questions and feelings? Who's been the narrator and observer of these things? Who is this witness within? Feel this as warmth within your own heart.

You are now sensing and in touch with the unchangeable inner self. Now, if you are ready, you can ask your higher self to have a greater say in your own life. It's the job of the continual inner self "I" to use the mind and body to serve the higher self in your lifetime. You can give your higher self a name if that feels right to you, like a friend you can call on for guidance whenever you want.

You don't have a Naphsha, you *are* a Naphsha. This quantum aspect of the true self resides both within you and in the field. It has constant access to the field of all potential and knows what outcome is best for you at this time. Imagine it as a source of all intelligence in the form of a ball of light that floats above your head with a channel flowing down through the crown chakra to the heart where the inner self "I" lives.

Say the following:

"I surrender my ego, my small thoughts, my limiting beliefs about what I deserve and what I am capable of. I clear all these now. I am ready for your guidance in my life. I ask that you direct my path and give me clear guidance through my internal guidance system and make it clear so I recognize and understand it. I trust that you will guide my life with your bird's-eye view far better than I have done with my ego's small view of yesterday. Make me a vessel of your perfect expression in this body in my life now for the highest good of myself, of humanity, and with ease, grace, and flow. Thank you. What I seek is seeking me. It is on its way to me now, and for that I am so thankful. I let it be so, and so it is."

Journal or create a vision board collage of how your Naphsha wants to express through you in this lifetime. FEEL this energetic way of being and begin to practice it.

Daily Mantra:

I AM MY I AM.

Chapter 5

Intention

"Nature abhors a vacuum."
~ Aristotle

Now that you are becoming freer and clearer, you can begin to replace what was once inside you with new healthier, soul-supporting, self-honoring thoughts and behaviors. You have created space within, and you may physically feel more spacious inside. This is the phase when people begin to seriously seek and do deeper work by going to new classes, having spiritual experiences, reading new books, or attending meditation retreats. You begin experimenting with living into the vision of how you see your life expressing itself.

You are planting seeds for the consciousness you are cultivating within you. You've become aware that the "I" is not a fixed thing at all but is rather fluid. There are many aspects to you, and yet deep within there is a constant hum of Naphsha. The thing you are seeking, however, is already within you. There is not a solid purpose, as in one thing you're here to do. That's entirely too stressful. It's about being in touch with the Naphsha that wants to express through you. It doesn't matter what you do—it's about who you're being while you do it.

This is where the power of intention comes into play. Intention is energy and it's the energy the universe responds to. Quantum science has shown that nothing happens without an observer. Everything exists in a state of potentiality until someone comes along and decides what to create. The observer creates the effect based on their intention. This makes measuring the stuff of the Universe impossible because it's everything until someone is looking!

Intention is the most powerful energy to master. Now that you have a vision of who you are capable of being, own the intention to become that, and the experience and its doors will start opening for you. It can be no other way. Always remember to check in with your Naphsha and your body to see if it's right for you.

The unconscious mind fuels most of your waking life without your awareness. Most people live on autopilot with old behaviors, thoughts, and feelings wired deeply within. So, don't be surprised when old ways of being resurface, because they will.

When old ways of being resurface as behaviors, you may give into them. As long as you're planting new seeds in your conscious mind, know that they are sinking deep into the soil of your unconscious mind. As you give in to your old habits, you'll find they're not as pleasurable as they used to be. This is an indicator that your vibration is changing. Ask yourself what you can do instead, and what better choice is more aligned with your intentional way of being. Then choose it next time the lesson presents itself.

Create an optimized space to help you resist temptation when it arises. And arise it will! When you have replaced negative habits with positive habits, you begin to see how good you feel living in integrity and alignment with your heart and higher self. Make it an *effort* to slip into old behaviors. If you must go out of your way to engage in an old behavior, then it becomes a conscious choice. Just know that when you give in, you are planting the same old seeds with the new ones, so behave with awareness. Consciously choose everything you do. Every choice you make rewires the neural structure of your brain.

Every time you say no to yourself (your low-vibe ego), you are slowly rewiring your brain. Know that the very act of awareness and choice is the work. Every shadow that comes up is asking for your own love and acceptance of it. You can talk to this part of yourself with kindness. "Yes, I see you. I used to do that, but I don't anymore. Thank you for helping me to cope when I wasn't aware. Now I am aware and I'm choosing to be in alignment with my higher self."

If you do slip into old behaviors, don't beat yourself up! Simply notice the experience, and if it isn't taking you in the direction of your vision and intention, you chose incorrectly to be in agreement with an old intention. Release it at once. Treat everything as information.

Replacement and Muscle Testing Practice

Get your journal and create a plan! It's super important to go slowly without changing everything overnight. You are a natural being who moves and grows at the pace of nature, and nature doesn't like rapid change. Change that happens fast in nature is destructive, so give yourself the gift of grace and space to allow the process to work in you, with you, and for you.

Look up "muscle testing" on YouTube or get a pendulum to use until you learn to understand the feelings and the knowing that comes from your body. Ask your Naphsha if this is what you are to do.

- Choose one thing you intend to replace, and choose one habit or behavior that no longer serves your soul's growth.
- If you are using muscle testing, ask if your Naphsha wants this for you. If you are using a pendulum, always ask it to show you yes and no and call in the love and light of your Naphsha before asking the question.
- Choose one thing to stop doing and one thing to start doing. Use a method of motivation that works for you—an X on a calendar, an app that tracks habits, etc. Don't try to change everything at once; keep it simple. For instance, I replaced

sugary goodies with fruit. My sweet tooth now gets a piece of fruit instead of a cookie.

- Know and say out loud, "Choice by choice I build my life. I now choose _____ instead of _____."

Notice how you feel when you make a self-honoring choice aligned with your intention. Tune into this feeling of integrity, gratitude, and self-respect. I can assure you that the Naphsha is very "blissiplined."

Chapter 6

Rewire & DOSE

"A mind stretched by new experience can never go back to its old dimensions."
~ Oliver Wendell Holmes

As I mentioned in the previous chapter on replacement, each time you say no to yourself you are rewiring your brain. Introducing new concepts and perceptions also rewires your brain. I am so grateful that the brain is plastic in nature and can be molded, shaped, and changed. Meditation is the key and the foundation of all lasting mental transformation. Meditation cultivates awareness. It creates a space between thoughts and reactions.

What I find fascinating is that Yeshua used the Aramaic word "touveyhoun" for what we know as the beatitudes. This word was interpreted as "blessed are they who" by the Greeks, but in the original Aramaic it means, "a neural structure that connects us to our Source." So, not only are we Naphsha connected to Source, but we also have the built-in wiring to connect us to Source. I believe it to be the pineal gland, a crystalline semi-conductor in the brain that converts sound into light in the mind and controls the hormones.

This means we need to learn how to use our brains for their intended function: to imagine and create in service of our Naphsha. When we tune into our third eye, we see beyond what the physical eye sees.

Mindfulness meditation can be done in many ways. You don't have to close your eyes and count your breaths to meditate. Any time you're aware that you're aware (metacognition), you are being mindful. If you have been doing these practices, you are certainly becoming very aware of your awareness.

Notice these moments of awareness and see how long you stay present before your mind goes time traveling into fantasyland again. Research has shown that as little as 10 minutes of meditation makes an enormous impact on the brain by changing the brainwaves of our busy gamma and beta states to the slower brainwaves of creative receptivity and relaxation found in the alpha and theta states.

I have a theory about what Yeshua meant when he said, "To get to the kingdom of heaven, be as little children." Children are in a theta brainwave state until around eleven years old. Theta is the brainwave state of spiritual connection, creative downloads, daydreaming, and imagination. They didn't know about the brainwave states two thousand years ago. They knew by experience and paying attention.

Rewiring your brain takes time, but it's the most important work you can possibly do to create a new way of habitually being present in the now to the world. We've already determined that who you are is up to you. At the beginning of changing behaviors and trying new things, a lot of conscious energy is required and yes, it's hard, even unpleasant. This is where the power of your vision and intention comes in. Let them be the guiding force and energy behind the *why* to rewire your brain. The job of the brain, the thinking mind, is to be in service of the awakened heart.

It's so important as you do the work of awakening to give yourself a DOSE of feel-good neurochemicals to keep you motivated. DOSE is an acronym for dopamine, oxytocin, serotonin and endorphins.

1. Reward yourself! Dopamine is the reward chemical in your brain. You stimulate it by accomplishing a goal you feel good about. Small wins are important. Getting enough sleep and

eating something delicious and healthy set off this chemical as well.

2. Oxytocin is the bonding chemical released through physical touch. Hugs and snuggling with a pet release oxytocin. Socializing and being with people you care about, and acts of kindness (even those just witnessed) release oxytocin.

3. Serotonin is the mood stabilizer and gets released with mindfulness, being in nature, being in the sun, or enjoying a healthy juice, since most of our serotonin is in the gut.

4. Endorphins are painkilling chemicals and get released through exercise, sincere laughter, drumming, dancing, and listening to music.

Ways to Formally Practice Mindful Awareness

I have a personal motto: stay in the day you're in. You now know that the mind likes to time travel and the ego likes to judge you. Cultivating awareness and attention can only happen now, in the present moment, where life is happening and where choice always resides. I already said in another chapter that the very act of practicing is transformation happening. It's like witnessing a rosebud opening to reveal the beautiful rose within. It's not perceptible in the moment, but if you use time-lapse photography you will witness the change as it happens.

Tune into your breath.
Tune into your heartbeat.
Notice how you feel physically:
What do you see? Smell? Feel? Hear? Taste?

Who is the observer noticing you and what you are doing? Who or what is the silent witness within? Listen within yourself and stay aware of everything in your surroundings. Play a game of zooming in and out. Awareness takes in everything. Notice all you can with your senses and then zoom in on one thing. This is attention, and this is the difference between awareness and attention.

You can play this game while cooking, walking, doing dishes, painting, dancing, people-watching, building something. Literally, anything you're doing can be used to cultivate and harness your powers of presence, awareness, and attention.

In doing this practice, you create a noticing awareness in your own mind. So, when old habits kick up again you'll be very aware of them, so you can choose something else. This is how you go from being reactive to responsive. I have heard that reactions are trauma coming to the surface. When you notice your body, and where you feel a reaction (re-acting) breathe into it. Soften. Release. Choose.

One day I noticed the spelling of "reactor" and said, "Hmm, a reactor is a creator who got all mixed up." I have been both, and I prefer being a creator.

Chapter 7

Tuning Into Source

"The Universe is conscious, expansive, and alive. Everything in the Universe is a vibration, and all that is, is in all that is." ~ Joya

Through the processes you've been practicing, meditation and cultivating self-awareness eventually lead you deep within yourself. These practices expand your consciousness beyond your own thinking mind. When you begin these processes you encounter the physical body, then thoughts and emotions. Finally, you arrive at a clearing where you ask yourself, "If I am not the body, not my passing thoughts and passing emotions, not the same person I was as a child or last year, or even yesterday, then who am I? What am I?"

The answer to that question is that you are an aspect of the Divine Source, which is everything and in everything. The Divine Source created and creates everything. It's not a person, not a human god on a throne with a beard as religion teaches, but rather it's an energy—a force as real as gravity. You have the presence and power of God in you. This creative, dynamic, expansive force is manifesting itself as you and expressing itself through you, when you allow it.

Consciousness is awareness, understanding, and knowledge of something. When you attune to this vibration of consciousness, of God as you, then you come to realize that how you've been living and what you've been creating is not even close to your potential as a creative being, a direct fractal of Creator consciousness!

Let's play a game of consciousness. Bring to mind a light pink daisy. Really visualize it. Smell it, feel it, see it. Close your eyes for a moment and use the imaging faculty of your imagination to see it.

Because you are aware of what a pink daisy is, you can bring it to your conscious awareness. If I asked you to imagine a flurple megididoff, you couldn't, because there is no such thing to reference, but you may notice that your mind will search for what it could mean, and start to make up a story; unless you're incredibly rational.

Now bring to mind the consciousness of your holy self—your Naphsha, the aspect of you that is always connected and in touch with Source. Visualize that you are a drop of water in the ocean. This means that the whole ocean is what you are a part of, that you have the power and elements of the ocean within you. This is the same as God source, Creator source. It is Divine creative energy that is true of you, in you, as you.

Say to yourself, "I am not all of God (or whatever you like to call this Source), but God is all of me." Again, you can use the ocean analogy if it helps with this understanding. "I am not all of the ocean, but the ocean is all of me."

You will feel a vibrational quality of truth resonate within you as you feel into this idea, especially if it is a new one for you. Ask your Naphsha to make itself even more known to you, to come into your conscious awareness, to help you see that this creative force is indeed all of you. You may feel a warmth in your thymus, the center of your chest. This is the heart chakra.

Be on the lookout for signs and symbols as a confirmation. They are the language of the human, and our Naphsha speaks to us in ways that we will understand. Look for a sign; it will arrive. Meditate daily on this idea and allow it to expand into your heart and consciousness.

1. Can you think of a time when you were sent a meaningful sign or symbol, that let you in on a cosmic secret of knowing you are heard and cared about? Was it a song? A word? Something

someone said? Did something appear and you just knew what it meant?

2. Try this now. Tune into that vibration within you and ask for confirmation that it's true. Ask that you be shown with ease and grace, one that you will undeniably understand.

3. Be open and on the lookout. Notice when it happens and when it does, tune into your Naphsha (your higher self) and with gratitude say thank you.

You Become What You Are Conscious Of: An Expansion Practice

Consciousness is awareness, understanding, and knowledge. When you begin to expand the consciousness of your Godself, you begin to envision even greater fulfillment of your being! These aren't steps you take in order, but rather steps you take in a spiral. The more knowledge and understanding you have that you are this source, the more expansive you feel in your innerverse—the universe within you.

- Here's a saying I love: "If you spot it, you got it." This means that anything you see in someone else you contain within you as well.
- Journal what it means to be a drop in the ocean, that God is all of you. What do you see that you couldn't see before that is possible for your life? Can you feel how sacred you are, that this light within you is to be cherished and loved?
- Think of all the qualities you love and admire when you think of the Source, Divine Creator. Write them down.
- After you've finished, ask someone close to you to tell you the qualities they see in you. How many of them match what you said about Source? How many match up to anyone you love, respect and admire?

- As above, so below. As within, as without. You spot it, you got it.
- Say thank you to the Divine within you, for bringing to your conscious thinking mind the beauty that it is and the possibilities that are waiting for you to align your vibration to be a match to them.

Chapter 8

Desire is the Secret

"Imagine the freedom you would have if you could totally trust yourself to only choose that which is in alignment with the desire and will of your Higher Self." ~ Joya, from my journals

Human beings choose nonstop, without even thinking about what choices are being made for more than a split second. You are choosing to read this book, and as you read these words you are choosing to believe them or not. You might choose to get up and get a drink or a snack. You might choose to take a walk. You choose everything, at every moment, including the thoughts you think.

That's why cultivating mindful awareness and attention is so important, so when you notice your thoughts are disempowering, you're free to choose differently. The most important step you can take as you open yourself up to your spiritual nature is taking responsibility for your whole self: thoughts, feelings and actions.

I like to spell it response-ability, or your ability to respond instead of reacting mindlessly over, and over, and over again, never aware that there's a choice in thoughts, emotions, or actions. For most people, trigger = reaction. Someone yells at you, you automatically yell back without thinking.

Choice originates at the point of desire. Without the energy of desire, nothing can happen. Desire is the energy that drives all action. Let's take a simple example. You think a bowl of ice cream sounds good. You get a desire for it, your body reacts to it physiologically because you can clearly imagine it with all your senses. This energy of desire motivates the body into action to create it in your material realm.

Creating anything is the same formula as creating the bowl of ice cream. The only difference is the level of consciousness, the difficulty in achievement, and the level of consistent action.

Your desires must align with your thoughts. There's a loop within the realm of the body: thoughts create emotions (energy in motion) which stirs up desires, desire creates intention which creates action, which creates results. Results feed thoughts, and back into the loop you go. So, it looks like this:

thought>feeling>desire>intention>action>outcome> feeling>thought> etc.

Therefore, it's important to guard your mind. Every spiritual teaching knows that the mind, the realm of thoughts, must have correct information flowing into it to create correct outcomes. The highest vibration, love, seeks to expand that which is like itself, which means that within you is the capacity to access this realm because it is within you, as you learned in the last chapter.

If you can get a sense that what you create in the world is based on what you desire, it's time to get crystal clear on what you desire, and make sure that those desires align with your highest good. The more your desires align with the highest good for yourself and for the highest good of all, the easier it is to create them. Desires based on the highest vibration of love are easier to manifest and create in your world because your spirit, an aspect of the one Spirit and one mind, knows what would be harmful to you and to others. If you say you want to create millions of dollars but your spirit knows the desire is based on greed, gluttony, or lust you'll have a more difficult time creating that reality. There will be more resistance.

1. Looking back at the vision you want for your life, what is it that you *truly desire* to create? If you said more money, is the desire really freedom?
2. What are the choices you must make to create that desire? Are there areas of conflict in what you think you desire vs. what you're choosing to do?
3. Knowing that you create what you truly desire. If there's a gap in your reality between conscious desire and action, that means there is a deeper, unconscious desire overriding your conscious desire.
4. Write down what's happening, what you're choosing at the choice point, and what's creating the unwanted results in your life.
5. Now, ask your Naphsha for strength and guidance to be aware at this choice point to choose with response-ability what your new desire is, and to let the old agreement be cancelled and cleared. Journal about any resistance you notice. There may be some shadow work (forgiveness) that needs to be addressed.

Slow Down and Ask Before Choosing

The more you begin to attune to your higher self and the wisdom of your Naphsha for the choices in your life, the more it will guide you to greater and greater choices, which create greater and greater outcomes. With much power comes much responsibility.

- How do you feel about taking responsibility for yourself? Are there any areas of your life that you feel deep down are not your responsibility?
- You must be willing to have everything in your basement (your unconscious) brought into the light to transmute and transfigure or to simply dissolve.

- This is not easy work, which is why most people are complacent to habit mind and the small self, ego-based comfort zone. How willing are you to stand in the power you have over your own dominion (your life), and to accept that the creations in your life are all based on choices you have made?

Most people react mindlessly to desire. As a desire arises, it sends the body into action mode and people slip into autopilot. Desire also has a shadow side in the forms of lust and greed. Lust isn't just sexual, lust is the desire to have your sense pleasures fulfilled, and people will gladly sacrifice what they really want for what they want right now. The TRUE desire is to feel better.

Guarding your mind and filling it with what you truly desire to create is a key to joyful life. You must train your mind to be a servant of your awakened heart, which desires to only know more and more of Source living through you as you. It is the desire of every human heart to return to Source.

A Simple Practice to Accept Your Choice and Creation Power

Notice when you are at a simple choice point, like choosing to brush your teeth, or choosing to make toast, or choosing to read this book.

Say out loud, "I am choosing this. My desire in choosing this is_____.

After you have completed the activity, notice the outcome. Clean teeth and fresh breath, a satisfied stomach, an expanded mind.

Say to yourself, "I chose that, and I created this outcome, and I am very satisfied with my results."

When you become a master of the little things, you will become a master of the bigger things. It's all the same thing in varying degrees and lengths of time to create. In practicing your choice of power over simple things, you build the muscle to have the discipline and stamina for the bigger things.

Remember that every choice, every moment, is practice. Your life is practice. You are living the answers to your desires. Everything you can conceive of already exists in The Field. It is up to you to claim it, choose it, be it, and create it.

Chapter 9

Receptivity & Having

"You cannot create what you will not graciously receive, allow, and accept into your consciousness." ~ Joya

How do you receive? Do you accept a gift, a compliment, helpfulness, with love, with ease, and with grace? The energy of receiving is like the energy of the soil opening to receive the seed being planted in it. You are both the planter and the receiver of what you are choosing to plant! The ability to receive is one of the most important and overlooked secrets of being the creator you truly are. So often people are handed what they asked for, only to turn it down or reject that it is meant for them. And you cannot have what you will not receive.

So, take a moment here to explore honestly. What is your mindset around receiving? Do you allow others to help you when they offer to? How do you receive something as simple as a compliment? Do you give more than you receive? Notice your receiving energy. Are there any blocked feelings of deservedness or worthiness?

Pay attention to opportunities to receive. Remember when I told you to ask for signs, symbols, and synchronicities? This is often the universe sending that sign or symbol and is a confirmation that you are indeed ready to receive what you desire to create in your world. Are you saying, "Yes, I receive this blessing?"

There are simple ways to practice receiving. Imagine that each time someone pays you a compliment, or offers to help, or offers to buy your lunch, you open yourself up like soil receiving a seed of love and worthiness and you say, "Thank you. I appreciate and receive that." The moment you open to receiving is the moment you no longer *need* anything because now you have it. The moment you receive with love, gratitude, and appreciation is the moment you move from lack to abundance, from wanting to having.

When you say to someone, or even to the universe that provides all the time, "Thank you, I receive that," you're acknowledging and imprinting a new reality and energy onto yourself. And you are giving a gift to the person giving! It's a joy to give as much as it is to receive.

In New Thought teachings this is called a demonstration. The more you practice noticing, receiving, and acknowledging the effects of choice, which come from the cause of you, the greater these demonstrations will become. This is about being so that you expect to receive what you are being in the world. It can be no other way!

Receiving Chases Away What You Don't Want

Humans get the process of creation so wrong. The more you focus and think about what you don't want to happen or focus on the energy of wanting and needing something, the more wanting and needing you create for yourself. The universe responds to your vibration, not just to your words. So, as you do this work of transforming from your ego-based 3D small self to your higher vibrational light body Naphsha self, the universe will send vibrations to check if there's resonance.

Graciously receiving and acknowledging what you desire rids you of lower vibrational creations.

Practicing the Energy of Receiving

- Journal about the energy of receiving and how it feels to you. If there are any blocks whatsoever, ask that they be revealed to you with grace and ease.

- When you ask, know that what you seek is seeking you in return, and be on the lookout for the answer.
- When you receive it, acknowledge receipt and attune to the loving vibration of your higher self, which seeks to manifest its grandness in your life, for the sheer joy of it.
- When you are in creation mode, practice receiving what you desire before you have it, knowing with total conviction that it is on its way to you now, and give thanks ahead of time that it is so.
- "I am so grateful to receive _____ now. I let it be so, and so it is."
- Then, when it arrives in whatever form, give thanks, and receive deeply.

Chapter 10

WORD POWER

Abracadabra: I create as I speak.

If you think, feel, and imagine something and you speak it, you just gave it a lot of power.

Have you ever noticed how much power people give to what they don't want? I've learned to listen a lot and keep my mouth closed and be very conscious of the power of words, because they are energy. You can't see it with the physical eye, but your words make an imprint on the quantum field of creation. Words are the blueprints of creation. If you listen, most people complain or talk about their fears or talk about what they don't want to happen, without realizing that giving it voice gives it more power to materialize it in their world. And so they create what they fear and don't even realize how powerful they are because they think it's something credible, or someone else's fault.

Words are decrees. "If you decree a thing, it is so." Everything we say sends out a vibration into the field. It creates a ripple seeking a return vibration. Words spoken with intention are a vibratory force. Abracadabra is said to be based on an Aramaic word that means, "I create as I speak." Think about the power of the words you use. Words can be used to build up or to tear down, to create or to destroy.

Words can be used, as we mentioned in Chapter Nine, to affirm to the universe that which you are visioning and receiving into your life. Every word is a container of meaning. A word is filled with the energetic intention of the speaker of the word. Think of everything you say as an affirmation. It's what you say and how you say it and what the intention is behind it. Words are not just words. The childhood poem "sticks and stones may break my bones, but words can never hurt me," is a total lie.

Feel the energy of these words in your body as you say them aloud: LOVE. What do you feel, what do you notice? What comes to mind? Now, HATE. What do you feel? What do you notice? What comes to mind? Love creates open expansive feelings, whereas hate feels closed off and constricted. This is your physical energy field giving you information about what expands you and keeps you alive, vs, what collapses in on itself. Have you ever had the experience of angrily telling someone off, and then you are the one who feels terrible? I sure have.

The power of affirmations is the power of words. You can use words to create and build your own life, and begin to give life to the vision, the desire, the intentions you have as the Divine Creator of your own life. Your mouth is between your head and your heart. Let your words reflect who you are in your heart. Let your words be used to help lift and build the kingdom of heaven on earth. Let your heart speak, and you will create vibrations of love and inspire people and the universe to help you achieve whatever it is you desire to achieve. Words return like boomerangs.

I AM Practice

Sit for a moment with your journal open and allow stream of consciousness writing to take place. This means writing without giving it any conscious thought—no editing, no judgment—just allowing whatever wants to come out to do so.

Make a list. I am _____ and write until you feel complete.

Now, speak out loud the I AM statements you wrote. Notice the difference between the written word and the spoken word. Are any of your I AM statements untrue? If they are and you said them, then say out loud, "Cancel, clear, delete." Then correct your statement out loud.

The word *amen* is ancient, and means *so be it*. It's a declaration of affirmation.

Let your words reflect your inner world. Your mouth and throat are the vibrational instruments of your soul, used to imprint onto the field that you are creating as a conscious creative chooser.

I let it be so. And so, it is. Amen.

Chapter 11

Being Your I AM Presence

"It is the science of the mystic, and it is the forte of the
self-realized man, who, having sought, has found himself to be
one with God and is willing to play his part."
~ St. Germain, St. Germain on Alchemy

You have worked more and more with these practices and ideas, and you come to the place where you realize there is no set self, that there is no "me" that is solid and constant, but rather you are a construct of memories, beliefs, ideas, feelings, and actions. You are free to change your identity, memories, beliefs, ideas, feelings, and actions at any time. You are a very powerful creator.

And yet, in the back of this changing self, you may have a sense of something that has been constant in you, a sense of I AM within you. You were introduced to it in Chapter Four. As you do these practices, your relationship changes.

Yeshua said that we are Naphsha, and that within us was planted a neural structure to keep us eternally connected to our Source, I AM. This I AM is who you really are. You are the universal source intelligence, individually expressed as you for a little while. And you came with a blueprint or design for your personality and archetypes to express through you.

Revisit the idea that God is all of you, but you are not all of God. Do you have a more embodied sense of this now? Your I AM is all-powerful. Getting in touch with this expansive, powerful energy within you will help you see all the blocks you yourself have created.

In the beginning, I introduced you to the saying I AM MY I AM. Quietly repeat this mantra now, feeling yourself open to the whole ocean within the drop of you. Feel the vibrational connection you have to your Source. Feel this connection in your heart. Feel the inner peace and calm.

Seek and You Shall Find

This is the promise: ask, seek, knock. (I love that the acronym is ASK). Ask and you will be answered. Seek and you will find. Knock and the door will open. This is a guarantee.

- **Ask** for your I AM presence to reveal itself to you. Ask for your ego to take a back seat to your I AM presence. Ask for your heart to continually be open.
- **Seek** first the kingdom of heaven. What does this mean? It means the answers to your questions! The ideal your higher self longs to live as is in your body. Seek to align yourself with who you truly want to be, and everything unlike that will be revealed for you to love, heal, and release.
- **Knock** means keep being persistent. You are gifted with free will, and spirit doesn't force anything. As the door opens, it's up to you how much and how quickly you want to step through.

Keep your mind on the highest ideals of your I AM presence and ask constantly for it to guide you with grace and ease. Otherwise, lessons will be sent that can be rather painful to get you to see and change your behaviors that are out of alignment.

Living as your I AM presence means that you are learning the formula, I call DIAS: desire, intention, allowance, and surrender.

Surrender is the final step of trusting that another higher aspect of you actually has your back. It doesn't care if you're famous, if you're rich, if you're thin enough, or have enough Botox. It cares that you listen, that you desire, that you intend to embody these ideals, that you allow them to inform your life, and now you relax and surrender in the bliss of being love in human form. You can express that love in a number of ways, using your values, gifts, talents, and abilities.

Revisiting What You Desire to Create

In this Divine design of "me," you get to impress upon the 3D world of form that which you want to create or express in this body in this lifetime. Your heart burns inside with a longing for expression. This expression feels like purpose in being, and its simple purpose is to express the fullness of God in you for the sheer joy of creating and learning soul lessons in the body. Your plans will change as you awaken deeper and deeper into this love. You will find yourself simplifying your life.

One of my favorite New Thought teachers is Florence Scovel Shin, who wrote *The Game of Life and How to Play It*. She described four categories to create your life in: health, wealth, love, and perfect self-expression.

1. **Health** – Your health is your physical, mental, emotional, and spiritual well-being. How do you envision your ideals in these areas?
2. **Wealth** – What does wealth mean to you? What kind of physical manifestations do you want to create for yourself in this area? Notice if you have any blocks that arise here. Know that you have the energy of nature and wild abundance within you!
3. **Love** – Romantic love, family love, and friendships. What does love look like for you? What do you want to manifest

and create in the realm of relationships for yourself? What is your ideal in love?

4. **Perfect Self-Expression** – How do you enjoy expressing your creative powers? Creativity isn't just art making. Think of Mother Earth as a massive 3D printer where you can create anything you can imagine. What are you creating? Are you on a stage? Are you dancing? Cooking? Gardening? Arranging flowers? Singing? Decorating? Are you an amazing mother? Do you run marathons? Are you bringing out the beauty in your surroundings and in others? There are infinite ways of being perfectly, divinely self-expressed.

If you have no idea what your talents, gifts and abilities are, you can take the character assessment at viacharacter.org which is one of my favorite coaching tools because it's backed up by a lot of science and research, and is very accurate. The other coaching assessment I use is the Gene Keys chart, which you can get for free at genekeys.com.

Chapter 12

Attitude Adjustment

"Your attitude, not your aptitude, determines your altitude."
~ Zig Ziglar

What is an attitude? An attitude is a mindset. Merriam-Webster defines it as, "a manner of thinking, feeling, or behaving that reflects a state of mind or disposition."

The instructions of Yeshua are clear: know your I AM presence, and then let your attitude reflect it in how you think, how you feel, and how you behave. Here we return to thought, feeling, and action again.

Universities everywhere study attitudes, and in particular, gratitude. Studies of gratitude have determined that people who live in gratitude are happier and healthier than people who don't feel or express gratitude. Do a search for "gratitude study" and you will find a lot of research about the power of gratitude.

Gratitude is the feeling of a joy-filled heart of praise and thanksgiving. Gratitude forms an energetic, high-vibe link between your thinking consciousness and your I AM consciousness.

In navigational terms, attitude provides information about an object's orientation with respect to the local level frame (horizontal plane) and true north. In this same way, your attitude determines your destination and is an indicator of where you're headed. Your destination is based on what you're aligned with. Your true north, your Naphsha, is your constant guide.

Your I AM presence is your true north. True north always keeps you aligned. It's the constant by which you can always check your alignment.

Gratitude, then, is the energy of the confidence and joy in a direction for you to aim toward.

You discovered the power of words in a previous chapter, and the invitation now is to give praise and thanksgiving in a total attitude of gratitude. Give thanks for what you are intentionally aligning and creating: the ideals you've been writing and envisioning throughout this book.

Gratitude Practice

Bring to your mind's eye the ideals you've created for yourself in the four creative action areas of your life from Chapter 11: health, wealth, love, and perfect self-expression. See and feel yourself having and practicing all these ideals now.

Having established the knowledge that your higher I AM self is now at work in you, through you, and with you bringing, creating, and opening channels for expressions of self to come to pass, give thanks!

- "I am grateful, thankful, and blessed that I am at work in my life now for my highest good and for the highest good of others."
- Feel the joy and praise of complete highest goodness in your life now.
- Quietly say, "Thank you, thank you, thank you. I see the magnificence of God at work in my life, and I am thankful."

This is the energetic go-to, your I AM, to open the flow for miracles to appear because you are doing the work to get out of your own way.

The Be-Attitudes

I am not going to go too deeply into the Be-Attitudes here, but they need to be mentioned. Yeshua gave these instructions on being to humanity. They are deeply important, and I am creating a course that will be finished by the time this book is published, so if you are interested in learning more, you can take a deep dive into the Be-Attitudes on my website. www.vibologie.com

In another chapter, I alluded to them with the word touveyhoun, which has been translated in Greek to mean "blessed are they who," but in the original language of Aramaic, it implies neural structure, a prewiring humans have within connecting them to Source that will guide you when they are active. If they are inactive and you follow the instructions, you will have access to more of your Naphsha, designed to increase human happiness and well-being.

That's so much more than "blessed are they who ..." As I write them I say, "Theirs is a heavenly connection and transpersonal state, those who ..." followed by the Aramaic instructions.

1. Theirs is a heavenly connection and transpersonal state; those who make a home in the rukha. The rukha is the force that encompasses all the powers of the universe: spirit, energy, wind, electricity. It's from this that the rukha d' koodsha springs, the Holy Spirit. To be at home in rukha is to breathe consciously, to adopt an attitude that your I AM has you, so you have no earthly worries. It's an active connection to the forces from God.

2. Theirs is a heavenly connection and transpersonal state; those

who are aware of their mistakes shall be eased of mental suffering. This is what the first few chapters of this book are all about: forgiving the self for being less than perfect, to realize that what has gone wrong was for the experience of learning lessons, so that they may not be repeated anymore. It lets you off the hook with the acceptance that life is about learning as you go. It's the feeling that comes after shadow work because you have seen and corrected your errors.

3.   Theirs is a heavenly connection and transpersonal state. Those who possess humility, the mental quality of perceiving and cooperating with the good desire of others, shall possess the right to inherit everything. Humility springs from the heart, and true humility is the knowledge that the same Divine Source that lives in you lives in everyone. It doesn't compare, doesn't judge, and doesn't desire to be seen as special or better than anyone else. It sees and approaches others with positivity, assuming the best in others. When you are truly humble you can never lack anything.

4.   Theirs is a heavenly connection and transpersonal state. Those who hunger for the attitude of truth and fairness between people shall attain it. The wisdom of the heart is always to seek harmony with others and seek to solve problems. This attitude creates harmonious consciousness among people.

5.   Theirs is a heavenly connection and transpersonal state. Those whose love is unconditional will live in uncondi-tional love. In Aramaic, the words here are rakhma love, which is unconditional love that doesn't ask or need anything in return and appears in your behavior and in how you treat yourself, and kooba love, which is love that wants to do good and sees others in a loving light.

6.   Theirs is a heavenly connection and transpersonal state. Those who have a purified mind will comprehend the Alaha, the source of all creation. This purification of the mind can only come through purification of the heart and letting the heart

rule the mind, not the other way around. Ego thinks it solved the mystery. The heart knows it's living the mystery. It's in this living that one can begin to comprehend.

7. Theirs is a heavenly connection and transpersonal state. Those who produce the peace and understanding of God's will through service shall be called God's heirs. Peace is the word shlama, which means in Aramaic to surrender oneself, to put down your guard, to take off your false masks of ego. In this authentic nakedness, humans can then serve one another, and in this spirit of service one finds the peace of God.

8. Theirs is a heavenly connection and transpersonal state. For those scorned for their justness, theirs is the kingdom of heaven. The kingdom of heaven is malkoota d' shmeya, which means a heavenly state in an earthly life. This is the courage to stand up for what you know through your being is right. It means you can't be shaken or taken down by anyone or anything outside of you. When you stand unshaken and can choose to respond instead of reacting, you exercise this neural structure and the reward is inner fortitude, peace, calm, and unshakable strength.

These are the eight additional attitudes you can repose in to live in your highest vibrational self.

Chapter 13

The Messy Middle

"Everything is a complete mess right before it's cleaned up."
~ Joya

I feel it's important to discuss the messy middle. As you begin to do this work—and it *is* work—the time comes for you to have to clean your house, both literally and figuratively. As you ask, claim, and align, everything that is out of alignment will come forward for you to see so you can clean it up.

This is an invitation to revisit the chapter on forgiveness. This isn't a formula that has a point A to point B and then you've arrived at the finish. It's really a spiral process where you keep coming back to the same places, except from a higher and higher perspective. This is not about beating yourself up, but rather about clearly seeing and acting. Your I AM self can't create through you if you don't act. The point is to bring your idea of heaven to earth, manifest. Not just in your fantasies.

This process is much like deciding to clean out your closet. First, you have to pull everything out so you can sort what to keep and what to donate. You make piles. You put some things back. While you're in this process it's a huge mess, but a mess for the purpose of a cleaner, neater, more organized closet full of things you want to keep.

The heart and the mind work the same way. Everything that is unlike love will come up for you to see. Two of my favorite teachers, Ron and Mary Hulnick say, "How you relate to the issue is the issue." I didn't know what that meant until I started to deeply do this work. The practice is the transformation.

What area is your spirit is calling you to clean up? You'll feel it through one of the internal guidance systems we discussed in Chapter Four. Take an honest look at your life. Where do gaps appear between your ideal life and what you're physically doing now? Commit to working on just one thing. Remember that this takes time, just as it takes time for a rose to bud and blossom. Movement happens through action, and small actions lead to massive changes.

If you've been using anything outside yourself to mask what needs work, this time of change can be shocking and downright painful. I used food, alcohol, and shopping to numb out and escape how I felt, and to escape what I knew needed work and cleaning up.

The first thing that needed cleanup was how I related to the over-eating and drinking issues. Then, when you stop the outer escapes, the ego may turn its wrath inward. Here's what my experience was with that: I would be going along nicely on track, then go out and party and drink too much, have hang-xiety for three or four days, start feeling better, get back on track, and a week later repeat the sequence. Then I'd beat myself up for drinking so much again.

When I stopped this pattern and the alcohol was gone with no excuse for not getting where I wanted to go, I was left with only myself. And the truth. Then the outer wrath turned inward. Luckily, I had all these tools to get myself through that dark night of the soul! I practiced a lot of self-love (noticing my thought processes and correcting them) and self-forgiveness.

The outer excuse was used to procrastinate or self-destruct, but when it's gone, you're left to face yourself. It can cause you to think, "I'm doing all this spiritual work, so why do I feel worse than I did before?" Know that this is just the messy middle. Some call it shadow work, but it's all part of the process of freeing yourself from your small-self ego that wants to keep you small.

1. Breathe. Give yourself grace and self-kindness. Ask your I AM presence to grant you peace in the cleanup process.
2. Know that every time you say no to your ego and its habits that keep you small and stuck, you're saying yes to your soul. Give yourself praise and thanks!
3. Don't worry about doing everything at once. Just commit to one thing at a time. If you're doing a big thing that was out of alignment, give it all the time it needs to heal and for new in-alignment habits to replace it.

The Messy Middle Space and Grace Practice

If you have ever deep cleaned anything you know what I mean by the messy middle. I used the closet analogy. When you clean a closet, you take everything out of it and sort it between what you're keeping and what you're donating. It's a mess, and this process is no different. But know that as you keep sorting, slowly but surely you're putting yourself back together again more organized, clean, and aligned to your I AM, to your ideals, and the fact that you're making self-honoring choices. Your Naphsha is showing you all the things that no longer serve you.

Transformation requires courage.

- When it's hard, give yourself space and grace. "Things are difficult right now, but I see and know the end result is on its way to me, just as I'm on my way to it. I'm thankful that it's on its way to me now! What I seek is seeking me and I'm making my way to it."
- I choose self-honoring behaviors and self-honoring talk as I skillfully navigate my way toward the light of my ideal life, created through my I AM self.
- This. Too. Shall. Pass.

- Do something that brings you joy, or if you feel like crying, cry. Journal, scream, let it out! I love to have my clients do a practice I call "sound it out." Just stand up, root yourself, call in your Naphsha and let yourself make whatever sounds you want to make. Let that energy move out of your emotional body where it's been living.

Chapter 14

Skillful Action

"Every action has an equal and opposite reaction."
~ Sir Isaac Newton's Laws of Physics

Every action has a pushback reaction. There isn't a single thing you do that doesn't create a ripple in the world. Every action is cause and effect. All you have to do is take an honest look at your life to see what kinds of effects you've created with your actions. Skillful action means that what you do is in alignment with what your ideal I AM self has gifted you to create in this world.

Skillful action means doing things with intention. If you do nothing, you get nothing. If you yell at someone, they will probably yell back (unless they are also practicing being in their I AM self.)

Patience is the other side of skillful action. Our whole world is an impatient society that wants satisfaction now. The problem with this is that *good things take time.* What is real and lasting takes time to cultivate and create. In many ways that's a good thing, because it gives you time to correct course and make sure that what you're creating is truly what you want to create.

If you're mindless you'll act out of momentary sense pleasures, rather than choose to act in alignment with your ideal life. You'll sacrifice what you really want for what you want right now.

Most people go through life trying to correct the effects (results) of their actions. The world of effects, what you've created right now, is the world of what's past. What you have now is the result of what you've already done. To get something different, you must begin to do something different now to create something different in the future. Most people look to the outer world of effect as the problem in their lives, rather than seeing that they're the cause, and the change has to come from the inside. This is like seeing your face is dirty, so you try to clean the mirror instead of washing your face. You cannot change anything or anyone around you to be different than it is. In fact, when you notice you are doing this, forgive yourself!

The world is a screen on which you create and project your creations. In *As You Like It,* Shakespeare said, "All the world's a stage, and all the men and women merely players." All the world is a stage, and you're the player, the writer, and the director of your own story.

Everything Does Not Happen for a Reason

I mentioned in another chapter how I dislike this saying, because it's not true. I want to say a little bit about trauma, violence, or tragedy you may have experienced. Everyone in this world has free will, and sometimes innocent people are hurt by the sleeping people who don't know that they, too, are an I AM presence. That's why Jesus said, "Father, forgive them; for they know not what they do." (Luke 23:34) They are asleep, and hurting people hurt other people because they project their own pain onto the stage of life. But the universal loving Creator put a force in the universe to reverse the effects of wrongdoing. The Holy Spirit, the force called rhuka d'koodsha in Aramaic. The force that makes goodness out of all things, in time. I talked about it in another chapter.

Know that very few things are personal, as we've discussed in Chapter Three (forgiveness). Can you imagine the pain a person must be in to mindlessly inflict pain on others? Their inner life must be a living hell.

All of this is to say that you don't have any control over what other people say or do, and sometimes you are negatively affected by a choice another person makes. There is, however, growth opportunities in these experiences.

There is a thing called post-traumatic growth. People who have been through painful, awful, soul-crushing experiences can come out stronger, more resilient, more loving, and compassionate. I know I did.

Know that the only person you have any control over is yourself, and you're letting that self be guided by your I AM self. Sometimes skillful action means waiting. It means being silent when you want to speak. It means walking away from toxic people. It means saying no to temptations, including those from your own ego.

Skillful Action Practice

The next time you're engaged in anything, whether it be cleaning your bathroom or painting a masterpiece, bring your attention and awareness to your movements, your intention behind the action, and acknowledge your mastery in action. Feel your skillful action expressed and, notice your skillful action turned inward in the form of blissipline.

Chapter 15

Alchemy

"Divine alchemy is the transmutation of the small ego self into the higher I AM self living as your Naphsha." ~ Joya

You may think of alchemy as the ability to turn lead into gold, but alchemy is the ability to turn your ideas and mental impressions into creations in your world. From this standpoint, *everyone* is an alchemist! But you, armed with the practices and knowledge in this little book, can stop creating small meaningless shadows and become the powerful creator your I AM Source is, and therefore you are.

You have I AM power. You have I will power. You have I do power.

These three powers, backed by unshakable faith, make you a force in the world. When you are aligned with your higher self, I AM power, you are a force for good in the world.

Your alchemy power is to be attuned to the link between spirit and matter. All laws are universal laws. Remember: as above, so below. There is nothing out there that is also not here. It is in the energy of belief and total faith that you become one of those that Yeshua said, "… shall do greater things than I."

All is mind, one mind, one substance. The same drop of ocean that you are is the same drop that everything is. This mind is mental and conscious.

This conscious mind responds to those who will to use it. The all is in the all, and is available to those who understand this principle. You, your I AM presence, is the I AM presence of God. You have untapped creative powers available to you at every moment.

Miracles are ordinary. The small self, the imprisoned self we have created, is not normal. Remember that every cause has an effect, and every effect has a cause. The laws will be used according to your own faith and beliefs.

Expand Your Creations

How are you using the laws? How are you putting into practice the wisdom in this book? What are you thinking about? What are you feeling? What are you doing?

- Expansion and success are the natural order of things. Nature is a reflection of the perfection of the I AM creator energy.
- Nothing is truly at rest. Everything is in a state of vibration. Everything is an energy field that is constantly attracting and repelling that which it resonates with.
- Do these practices to come into resonance with your I AM presence. Think, feel, and act in alignment with your ideal I AM self. Know beyond a shadow of a doubt that you are a Divine expression of the God Source, just as a drop is an expression of the ocean.
- Know that to create and manifest in this world is to put in physical energy, in vibrational alignment to who you are being.

Ask and it shall be given. Expect it. Say I AM MY I AM with feeling, conviction, reverence, and love. Know beyond a shadow of a doubt that you are a living, breathing, moving force of the energy of Divine love. So, the spiritual work means everything unlike that energy will come to the surface for you to cancel, clear, and delete. It's not an easy path at first. But once you do this work and continue to do it, more and more and more will be revealed to you.

Yeshua said, "To those who listen to my teaching, more understanding will be given, and they will have an abundance of knowledge. But for those who are not listening, even what little understanding they have will be taken away from them."

Ignorance is not bliss. A person can spend their whole life sweeping things under the rug, keep tripping on the rug, and choose to never clean it up. These are the people who come to the end of their physical incarnation and are filled with the ultimate regret: the regret that it really is too late to do all the things the Naphsha wanted them to do. They ran out of time. Time's up.

You will discover the ultimate paradox as you do this work deeply. The more you become your Naphsha, the I AM presence, the more powerful you become, and the less you will want material things. They become frosting on the cake of life, not the meaning. You can create material wealth for the purpose of expanding the kingdom of love.

You will find that as you lose more of yourself, you will find more of you. As you become more and more of who you are, you realize more and more the *we* of all of us. This is how we all truly create community. A community is made of individuals, and a community of awakened humans serve each other, respect each other, and have peace, even if they don't agree on something.

Above all, as you do this work know that there is no *there* to get to. It's all about the journey, the growth, and the transformation into more joy, purpose, power, peace, presence, freedom, and abundance than you can even imagine right now. To live fully expressed is to continue to answer the call of what is calling you forward. Keep growing. Keep expressing. There is only one you.

I leave you with a blessing and a mantra:

May you open you and be liberated from all suffering, expand your consciousness, and allow your Naphsha to live and express through you in perfect peace and joy.

The Divine love of God IS the Source of me. I AM this Source expressing as myself. There is nothing I cannot do. I AM MY I AM.

And so, it is. Amen.

I have created a course to go along with this book that includes exercises using sound & vocal empowerment to assist you in raising your vibration. This is a free gift to you and is available on my website: www.vibologie.com

About The Author

Joya Sosnowski, MMT, B.Msc., is a transformational leader and visionary in the world of healing arts and mindfulness. With her diverse background in sound healing, spirituality, psychology and mindfulness, she has become a trusted resource for individuals seeking personal growth and transformation. A certified USM Spiritual Psychology Coach, a Mindfulness trainer, a Health Rhythms Facilitator, and a UCLA-trained Mindfulness Trainer, Joya has dedicated her life to empowering others to find their own inner strength, resilience, and joy.

As a survivor of severe childhood trauma and a suicide attempt, Joya is passionate about helping others break free from their own traumatic stories, limiting beliefs and false identities. She uses sound, art, vocal empowerment and drumming to facilitate transformational experiences for her clients, freeing them from stored trauma, false beliefs and limitations that stand in the way of self-mastery and self-expression.

A gifted sound healer and accomplished painter, Joya continues to expand her knowledge and expertise by studying with master sound, voice, and drum practitioners around the world. She is also a Gene Keys Guide and creator of "Be Artful & Mindful," a mindfulness program for those who struggle with meditation.

She is the founder of Vibe Raiser, whose mission is to inspire 1,000,000 voices to raise the vibe to love through chant and dance. As the host of "We Woke Up Like This," Joya is a guide for those who are on the journey of awakening to their true self.

Joya, also known as "The Vibologist," resides in Phoenix, Arizona, and is a light in the world, inspiring others to find their own inner strength, resilience, and joy. **www.vibologie.com**